The Journey
A Nomad Reflects

JOHN A. BRENNAN

ISBN-10: 0692500944
ISBN-13:978-0692500941
Library of Congress Control Number: 2015948099

DEDICATION

1   It's in the Genes

Geneticists, working out of Trinity College in Dublin, have recently discovered that the Irish gene pool is the least diluted in all of Europe, and perhaps the world. They have also found that the Irish traveling people (*tinkers) are purely Irish and date back to the nomadic hunter gatherers who inhabited Ireland beginning at the end of the last ice-age, prior to the arrival of our first named visitor, Cessair. The earth shattering discovery of the *Fox P2* gene, which is high in the Irish DNA, has been found to control the ability to absorb and internalize information, then, after formulating, express it using the voice. This particular gene is also present in songbirds, and serves to remind us that despite what the naysayers and begrudgers have said about us down through the centuries, we Irish truly are, a race apart. There's no-one else like us, period.

My Mother Ellen O'Connor was born in Kilmallock, Co. Limerick. My father Malachy Brennan was born in Crossmaglen, Co. Armagh. I was born in Croom. Co. Limerick, the home of the *Maigue poets*, and educated and raised in Crossmaglen, County Armagh.

Note* The word *tinker* is short for *Tinsmith*, meaning those with the ability to work with metals.

2   The Fox the Bird, and the Poet.

In the age when the Maigue, flowing broad from the Shannon, winding slow through the *sloping place* of Crom Dubh, right there, right on that spot, it all changed forever. For it was there that the Long-ships carrying the sons of Thor along its' looped course, stopped below the fastness sited high above the grassed banks, and sent the Linnet skyward from the heather, in frightful flight. And it was there, right on that spot, where O'Donovan parleyed, swore fealty and ruled in safety with the invasive Dane. And it was there that O'Connor encircled the ramparts at Rathmore, burned the enclosures and routed the pretenders. And it was there that the Norman puppet masters, with their Welsh and Flemish bowmen in tow, installed the Geraldines to rule in lieu. And it was there that Red Hugh, after the night time march across the frozen bogs, en-route to meet the Spaniard, met first with the Countess from Kildare. And it was there too that the hedge masters of Kilmallock gathered and birthed the written and spoken native tongue. Thus it was that the *Fil Na Maigue* rhyme was infused with life's breath and it was then, right then, on that very spot, in that very place, that the *Limerick* was born.

3   The Birth of the *Limerick*

The two founders of the Maigue Poets in Croom were Sean O' Tuama and his friend Andrias MacRaith. Both men grew up together in Kilmallock, Co. Limerick. O'Tuama went on to become a publican. After the two men had a falling out they began castigating each other in rhyme. Below are believed to be the first *Limericks* written, and predate Lear by one hundred years.

O'Tuama wrote:

"I sell the best Brandy and Sherry
to make all my customers merry.
But at times their finances
run short as it chances.
And then I feel sad, very, very."

MacCraith replied:

"O'Tuama, you boast yourself handy,
At selling good ale and bright Brandy,
But the fact is your liquor
Makes everyone sicker
I tell you this, I, your good friend Andy."

Dedicated to the Maigue Poets of Croom.

To Write Is To Live One's Dreams

Escribe Publishing Inc.
New York, NY

www.escribepublishing.com

ACKNOWLEDGEMENTS

I could never have attempted to write this book without the help of many individuals both living and long departed. My earliest influences were the men in the middle of the 5th. Century AD, the monks and scribes, who, against all odds had the foresight and tenacity to painstakingly collect, translate and record for the future generations the ancient manuscripts not destroyed in that brutal period of history known as the *dark ages*.

I owe a great debt of gratitude to the *Seannachie* (storyteller) tradition of the spoken word, which has transcended the ages and mists of time. I am proud to follow in their footsteps.
To the Irish writers Shaw, O'Casey, Synge, Wilde, Joyce, Swift, Kavanagh and Heaney a heartfelt thanks for paving the road.
To the *Maigue Poets of Croom*, County Limerick, Ireland, who, in the 19th century, kept the spirit of the written and spoken word alive despite the inhuman oppression brought to bear by the harsh invaders.

A special thanks to my fellow writers, poets and performers on Long Island and New York City for their inspiration, friendship and encouragement.

And to Malachy McCourt, John Kearns, Mark Butler, and the Irish American Writers and Artists, New York City, a special nod for their stellar efforts in keeping the spirit of the Bards and Minstrels alive.

INTRODUCTION

The Poet

If you were one of the inquisitive onlookers in Dublin on that fateful day in April 1916, and if you were close enough, you couldn't fail to see the lone figure, silhouetted by the light of the still raging pyre that was once the splendid edifice, the General Post Office. There, between two of the large, bullet shattered Ionic columns that supported the Greco/Roman pediment above the entrance, his broad brimmed fedora set at an angle over his brow, his tunic, dusty, torn, and bloodstained, right there on that spot, stood a poet. You would be forgiven if you were not aware that the poet was about to write his final stanza and immortalize a centuries old dream. If you looked closer still you would have been struck by the fact that although gaunt, disheveled, and shell-shocked, the poet's eyes still shone with the fierce brilliance of determination.

Adjusting his hat, and straightening his holster, he looked across O'Connell Street and focused on the imposing figure of the Admiral, atop the tall, granite pillar. *Ah. Horatio, I'll soon be joining you.* Then turning, he let his gaze linger on the bronze, sculpted figure that stood at their command post in the center of the building. The sculpture, of the ancient warrior, *Cu Chulainn*, was one of the poet's mythical Irish heroes and source of inspiration. *Cu Chulainn*, depicted tied to a pillar, at his own request, is slumped in mortal agony, his head hung in glorious defeat, the shield falling from his grasp, yet still, his sword is still clutched tightly in his right hand. A raven, with talons gripping the flesh on his shoulder, mirrored the poets deepening sense of foreboding.
The hounds have cornered me too, Setanta.

Turning toward the street once more, he scanned the faces of the assembled throng. *How many of them will remember. Will they one day understand that we did it for them?* The soldiers forming the cordon, their bayonets fixed, stared at him with unbridled, snarling contempt. He was taunted with shouts of "Bloody rebels. Traitors. Fenian bastards. Shoot them. Shoot them all." The poet waited calmly for the uproar to subside, then, when it was silent, he stepped forward, removed his belt and holster and handed them to the British officer. And thus it began and a terrible beauty was born.

Six days earlier, on Easter Monday, April 24, the poet stood on the same spot. His uniform was clean and neatly pressed the night before. His long greatcoat, with the sunlight reflecting off the two rows of brass buttons, dazzled the spectators, and forced those nearest him to shade their eyes. His revolver, holstered on a broad belt around his slim waist was loaded and tested. His eyes flashed with fervor in the knowledge that he was about to make history. In his right hand he held a rolled up parchment, his nation's destiny. Stepping forward, he opened the document and began to read. If you were still there and listened, really listened, you would have been awed by the poet's passion and conviction…

The poet's name was Patrick Henry Pearse and what he dared to read was the *"Proclamation of the Irish Republic."* At four minutes past noon on 24 April 1916 - Easter Monday, in a steady, forceful voice, and calling on his ancestors for courage and strength, he proclaimed once and for all time, freedom for his country and her people.

For Padraig H. Pearse

Weekly Irish Times, Vol. 44.02,078. Patrick Pearse, April 29, 1916
Web. 18 Sept. 2015. http://centenaries.ucd.ie/1912-1923-timeline/timeline-1915/patrick-pearse-licensed-under-public-domain-via-wikimedia-commons-2/.

TABLE OF CONTENTS

THE JOURNEY

A Nomad Reflects

By John A. Brennan

1

ON IRELAND

I start this book with a poem inspired by the works of W B Yeats, arguably one of the greatest Irish poets of the twentieth century. My writing has always been greatly influenced by the Irish writers Shaw, Wilde, O'Casey, Joyce, Synge, Swift, Pearse, Kavanagh and Heaney, whose works have prompted me to pick up the quill and follow in their footsteps. I dedicate this collection to them in thanks for the joy and inspiration they have given me through the years.

The Night Moths

I went down to the cool, dark woods,
when night moths were on the wing.
On earthly ghosts and raging floods
embraced my lonely pondering.
Moss clung fast to an olden tree,
near bank of river flowing slow
Salmon leap I smiled to see,
in silence, with a young moons' glow.
Fawn eyes bright, shone out at me,
from in the depths, and to and fro.

She licked my hand, while nestling free,
her tale to tell of the long ago.
She told to me, through cool night air
that time and space are here and now.
Spoke to me of a maid so fair,
with haunted look on her pale brow.
An apple blossom in her hair,
she haunts the woods in search of him.
To heal her heart and her love fair,
and cease the lonely wanderin'.
All at once near a white oak tree,
a girl in shimmering bright light,
came out and gently called to me.
Then both did meld, into the night.

For WB Yeats.

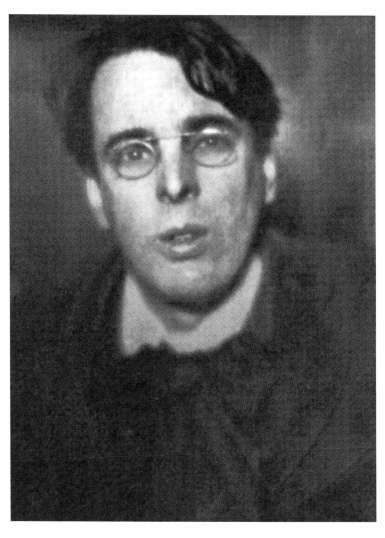

Coburn, Langdon. W.B. Yeats. January 24 1908. Web. 05 May 2014
http://digitalgallery.nypl.org/nypldigital/id?483420.

Ireland emerged slowly from the death grip of the last ice-age around 10,000 years ago. The land bridges which connected it with its nearest neighbors, England and Scotland, vanished as the vast ice sheets melted. A tale is told of the arrival of Cessair, a daughter of Noahs' son Bith and his wife Birren, just prior to the great deluge. She is said to be the first named individual to arrive in Ireland and was buried on the summit of Knockmaa, which is located south east of Tuam, in county Galway.

The First One

Cessair did come with fifty men,
to County Cork one fine spring day.
The ice had gone from off the glen,
ten hundred years, now long astray.
The flood to flee and its huge swell,
no room upon the ark, they say.
Were kin of Noah, so they tell,
left Bith and Birren far away.
Sailed the seas for seven years,
a deluge would sweep all life away.
Heart sore, spent and full of fears,
a green land beckons, this fine day.
A land of mists and young oak tree,
with lake and hill in future time.
Fleet fawns wild, and running free,
it's empty now, but soon will shine.
Some will take it, as if their own,
others more kind and loving be.
More will raze it down and burn,
the deaf ear hard, the eye not see.

The Singing Bones.

Inside my father's bones lie a million secrets.
Secrets passed down the long chain from the
beginning of time and the vastness of space.
In the glorious mix of diversity, endlessly
coursing through the shrouded mists of the
Holy Island, he breathes still. The memories
of his people, absorbed by the stones and the
very earth herself, exhale all that ever was.
Their essence still permeates, insisting that it
be never forgotten.
From Cessair, through Fomorian,
Nemedian, Fir Bolg, Tuatha, Milesian,
Celt, Viking and Norman, I inhaled that cocktail of life
with eager lungs and magnificent surprise.
I am inside my father's bones and my father
is inside mine.
He is the beggar-man, the holy man, the master
and the freeman. He still walks the fields, sure of foot.
He still wades the stream, fearless. He still lures the
trout, with quiet assuredness.
He still charms the goldfinch from her tree-top
perch, ever gently.
His bones sing loud enough for me to hear
even in the darkest, deepest reaches of the
night. On a quiet evening, I still hear his melodic
whistle floating on the air, calling to me.
Yes, I am inside my father's
bones, and he is inside mine.

Dedicated to my father Mal.

Photo of Mal supplied by Author

JOHN A. BRENNAN

The Green Valley

I've been down in the green valley: the holy place.
The one where pagan and saint walk the blessed
earth yet still, in silent mystic.
The one where the river flows ever onward to its birthplace,
carrying the tortured history, winding slow with measured
precision, to cast upon the ocean. Down where the sacred
hills, those silent sentinels to the glorious, tragic past,
keep watch in painful solitude.
Down where the spirits keen and await each dawn with
hopeful intent of peaceful morn. Where the lonesome,
royal fort is no more, the ramparts trampled roughshod
and buried underfoot.
Down where memories of olden kingly splendor died 'neath
the invaders harsh heel.
Down where the royal plain stretches, forlornly grasping
at the distant, unreachable horizon.

Down where the stone of destiny sits in erect remembrance,
remembering. Where ancient *Brehons*, in
their yellow robes, inscribed the laws of the common man
in flowing ogham script. Where the magicians cast the spells
of the *Tuatha* and conjured up the *Fianna*, the young ones,
the ones who would fight to save them.
Down where the sacred mound exhales the essence of all
that has gone before, and inhales all that will ever be,
the inscribed stones ever alive. Down where the sun aligns in
glorious magnitude within the cloistered, chambered walls.
Down where the haunting, haunted battle cries beseech
the blooded banks and echoes among the reeds and rushes.
Down where the lark soars straight as a fletchers' creation,
upward, up to the blue heaven, and sings.

Down where the final slaughter reached it's bloody, brutish,
climactic end on the plains of royal Meath.
The old King gone, the planted pretender crowned with a
foreign, alien hand, the scepter cursed.

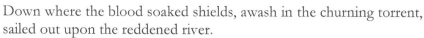

Down where the blood soaked shields, awash in the churning torrent,
sailed out upon the reddened river.
Down where the fields absorbed the crimson life force of the
vanquished, grotesquely strewn, dead, in furrow,
bracken and tussock.
Yes, I have been down in that green valley.

For all who went before.

Atop the mystical hill of Tara stands the stone of Fal, otherwise known as the 'stone of destiny.' There, through the ages, all Ard Ri (high kings) were crowned. Marriage ceremonies took place there also. These rites were always blessed by the Druid, the holy man of the Celtic peoples. The Brehons, (law makers) dressed in their yellow robes, made these rituals binding. Across the glen and over the winding river Boyne, is the sacred mound of Newgrange, 'bru Na boine.' This area is held sacred until the present day. The claddagh ring is a mystical symbol representing love, friendship and fidelity.

The three poems that follow tell the story of the union between the Master (the Druid) and his bride (the Druidess.) We travel with them to the sacred hill and observe the ancient marriage ceremony. We follow as they make their way across the river valley to the holy mound, and observe as they present their offerings to the ancients. We watch, from a distance, in silence, as they enter the cool forest to spend their first night alone, as man and wife.

The Hill: The Marriage

On Tara's sacred hill are found,
in unison and heartfelt troth.
A pair of old true lovers bound,
by brehon law and Celtic knot.

The spirits gather all around,
with their power they now instill.
In moonbeam bright and clear starlight,
two claddagh rings fulfill.

He holds her to his beating heart,
and swears his love this night.
The maid she swears they'll never part,
evermore will their souls take flight.

They walk across the valley floor,
to the mound above the Boyne.

And offer there to ancient yore,
their souls and hearts and minds.

A saddled mare for them awaits,
in patient silence and to greet.
This pair who here have coupled fate,
together now, night bound and fleet.

Ianfhunter, Stone of Destiny – Hill of Tara. September 13 2014. Web. 05 May 2015.
https://commons.wikimedia.org/wiki/File:Stone_Of_Destiny_-_Hill_of_Tara.jpg.

Newgrange is a passage tomb in the Boyne river valley in Ireland. It was built long before the pyramids in Egypt and is a sacred site. Erected in such a way that on the solstices, the sun's rays penetrate the light box above the entrance and fill the passageway and inner chamber with light. The ancients believed that the souls of the departed, represented by their ashes, which they placed in stone urns in the inner chamber, were taken by the retreating rays and transported to the afterlife.

The Solstice: The Offering

From the stone of Fal on Tara high,
'cross the river that flows deep and slow,
the ancients all gather at this holy place
to catch the bright morning's warm glow.
In robes of pure white, they walk the ground
and wait for the rising sun.
In the heart of the mound, old souls can be found;
heaven bound, they now become one

The Master appears, an unearthly sight,
and raises his arms to the sky.
The people bow down, and kneel on the ground,
then chant with a joyful cry.
The rays creep across the hills and the glen,
and strike the box over the door.
They follow along to the chamber, and then,
the love there enshrined, proudly soars.

It has always been done in this very way,
and for eons will last evermore.
Their spirits will rise and fly every day,
and watch over our true heart's core.

Karsina, Allen. Newgrange Tomb Entrance. 8 October 2006
Web. 23 Sept. 2015. https://commons/wikimedia.org/wiki/File.NewgrangeTombEntrance.jpg.

The wedding had taken place on the sacred hill and offerings were placed in the sacred mound. The couple then rode to the forest to spend their first night together as man and wife.

The Enchantress: Consummation

They used to say she was different, and not of their world, this strange woman of the forest. She spoke gently to the animals and they responded with affection. Of earthly treasures she cared not a whit. Always in commune with her surroundings, she walked her *chosen*, winding pathway with assured steps.

At the stream in the glow of an early moon, she disrobed and immersed in the cool, healing waters. As the water caressed and washed over her, she shivered and thought of the Masters' touch.
Her body, now in its primal state of openness, her tongue tingled with that familiar sense of desire.

As she submerged, her wild, dark mane floating on the surface, glistened in the soft light. Fawns, gathered along the banks to watch and protect, reflected her image in their large, sloe shaped eyes.
When she stepped out of the waters, she spread her arms, threw her head back, and with the moon rays caressing her, she sang.

 Low voiced at first, her sound became louder and soon soared upward on the night air. She had become the *Enchantress*.
Gathering the leaves and herbs from the trees and bushes, she anointed her body with their scented juices. She was ready to go to him knowing he would be waiting. He was all that she desired.

He was prepared to die for her love. Their union had been blessed by the learned men on the sacred hill, and now, their marriage would be completed on this night, in the forest.

Pyle, Howard. The Enchantress Vivien.1903. Web. 30 Jul. 2015.
https://commons.wikimedia.org/wiki/File:Author-Pyle_The_ Enchantress_Vivien.jpg.

The Night Ride

I saddled up a fresh young mare

rode through the night without a care.

O'er hills and fields and far away

rode her hard till the break of day.

Stopped off next to an old oak tree

where my own true love I chanced to see.

"Is that you William?" she waved and cried,

"I feared that you had surely died?"

"Not me," said I, my head held high,

"From the gallows tree I swiftly fly.

They won't catch me on this fine day."

Then he swept her up, up and away.

JOHN A. BRENNAN

In memory of my ancestor William Brennan (Brennan on the moor) who chose to become a highwayman after his forebears were ousted from their ancestral home in county Kilkenny, during the Norman invasion of Ireland in 1147.

The Rapparee

He rode from high to the valley floor,
and hid behind the old Rowan tree.
It was time to settle a deep-set score
and seek vengeance for his family.

They took the land, they took their pride,
rode roughshod o'er the scattered bones.
With mace and mail from far and wide,
castles shook, to the bare keep stones.

But now 'midst leaves, and masked and still,
flintlock and cutlass tried and true.
A glossy mare to do his will
those in league, are now sure to rue.

Coach rims crunch on graveled base
two pairs snort, wild manes aquiver.
He spurs her on, now quick apace.
"Halt there coachman. Stand and deliver!"

Goya, Francisco, 1786-1787, Asalto al coche. Web. 3 Aug. 2014.
https://commons.wikimedia.org/wiki/File:Asalto_al_coche.jpg.

Ask not why: (Lament for an Irishman.)

Ask not why those shots rang out, their retort
echoing across the crowded Plaza.
Ask not why those bullets coursed through the
warm Texan air, to strike with measured,
deadly precision.
Ask not why the smell of cordite invaded
the senses and stung the innocent eyes.
Ask not why the dreamers are besieged by
those who would conspire.
Ask not why their urge to drown potential
in the abyss of negative thought,
word and deadly deed.
Ask not why the inner light is detested and
feared by the forces of darkness.
Ask not why the lesser men are loosed in
time to hate all; to undo what was almost complete.
Ask not why the lamb was slaughtered in the arena
by the ungodly, his blood congealed in the sawdust.
Ask not why the faceless brood bayed with savage,
inhuman lust for his life force.
Ask not why the contorted, brutish minds always
justify their twisted tenets.
Ask not why evil holds its sway in a vise like grip
with the tenacity of the hellish beast.
Instead ask how.
How do we ensure that it does not repeat?
Ask how. How can we keep his message of hope
and optimism alive?
Ask what. What can we do for our country, our world?
Ask when. When will we see the likes of him again?
Ask where. Where do we begin?
Remember, remember, lest we forget the greatness
coldly stolen from us.

For JFK

Portrait of John F. Kennedy, President of the United States

Hunger

We, in this century, have the capability of producing enough food
to feed everyone on the planet and have a surplus.
With more *compassion* for our fellow man, no-one would or should
ever have to suffer the pangs of hunger. It is up to us to ensure that
food goes to those unfortunates whenever and wherever it is needed.
Compassion is the key.

Hunger is the physical sensation of a desire for food.
A desire for sustenance to nourish the body.
If this desire is not fulfilled the body will die.
It will die a slow, agonizing death.
The body will become a cannibal and consume itself
from within, in a futile effort to stay alive.
Then it will die.

Malnutrition occurs when the body is denied
the nutrients necessary to sustain life.
Starvation is the state of exhaustion caused by
the lack of food.
Famine is the widespread scarcity of food
caused by any number of events including war,
extremes of weather and political machinations.

The human, in the throes of starvation, will eat anything
including bark from trees, his own shoes, rats, insects and
even his fellow man. In Ireland during the great Hunger of
1847 starving people ate the grass at the sides of the roads. This
became known as *Green mouth* death.

In that same year the Cherokee and Choctaw tribes, just prior to
their enforced re-settlement in Oklahoma, had the *compassion* and
willingness to help the starving people in Ireland. Somehow, against
all odds they managed to send food and anything else they thought
would be of benefit, to save lives. Their journey became known as
the *Trail of Tears*. On that lonesome trail untold numbers of their
people perished from hunger, starvation and disease.
Let us end hunger now.

Doyle, Henry. Emigrants Leave Ireland. 1868. Web. 15 Jun. 2014.
https://en.wikipedia.org/wiki/File:Emigrants_Leave_Ireland_by_Henry_Doyle_1868.jpg.

A tribute to a kindred spirit, musician, poet, soldier and much, much braver man than I. Irishman, Bobby Sands, adhering to the ancient Brehon Law of Fasting, took his last breath in Long Kesh prison camp, on 5/5/1981. He survived sixty-six days without food or water while on hunger strike for his political beliefs. He was just 27 years old.

Bobby

The stone cold slab bruised hungry bones,
as he lay on the floor all alone.
His life ebbed nigh, but his spirit held high, as soon he would feast
with his own.

The visions he saw, the hope that he felt,
would never be taken by force.
His will was complete, his heart, one last beat, now the *way*, he would
lead to the source.

Asking, "Why, oh why did you have to die
on this accursed foreigner's floor?"
Saying, "It has to be me, so it will not be you,
Now, I'll go and throw open the door."

The piper's lament is heard in wide space,
as the warrior was laid in his grave.
The lark soared high in a sorrowful sky,
as he left us to join with the brave.

Baumann, Olaf. Bobby Sands Wandmalerei in Belfast. April 17 2006. Web. 23 Jul. 2014.
https://commons.wikimedia.org/wiki/File:Bobby_sands-wall_mural.jpg.

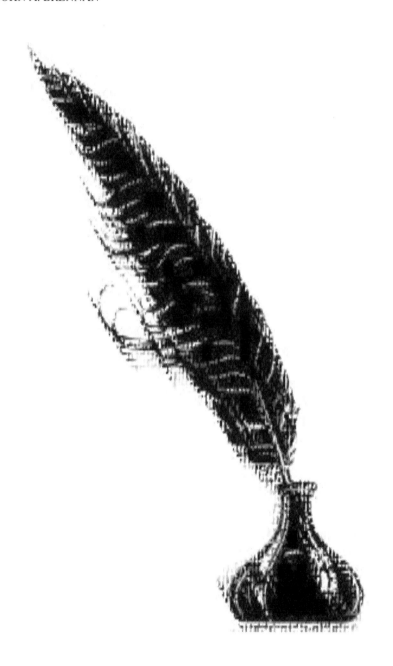

2

ON WRITING

The Writer

The writer, when the compulsion to write gnaws at his very marrow, and invades his senses with that unforgiving, ruthless relentlessness, will write. Nothing or no-one will deter him. He will retreat and seek solitude in the forest shadows or he will climb the summit of the nearest crag or he will huddle, cold and wet, in a stone hut on the bleak moor. No matter what his immediate surroundings be, he WILL write. He MUST write. He can't NOT write. Even confinement in a prison cell, wrapped in nothing but a blanket, will not stop him. He will write on anything available to him, walls, slate, clay tablets, animal skin, and the palm of his own hand… he will even write on cigarette papers.

Have you ever been to Mars?" I was asked one morning at two o'clock as I made my way up east Eighty First Street in Manhattan. I was returning home from a night out at Manny's Car Wash, a blues bar on Second Avenue. I stopped and heard it again, louder this time, "Have you ever been to Mars?" Looking around I couldn't see anyone and was beginning to wonder if perhaps I needed to have my hearing checked. Peering intently at the wall on my right, I noticed something move in a darkened doorway. Moving closer, I could make out the outline of a huddled figure lying there. As I got nearer I saw that it was a shabbily dressed man with long, unkempt brown hair and a beard.

A dirty plaster cast covered his right arm from shoulder to wrist. "Are you alright?" I asked. "Can you help me to get up?" was his reply. Grasping his left arm I pulled him upright and held him until he steadied himself. As his face came level with mine, in the eerie yellow light of the streetlamp, I was startled by the brightness of his clear, piercing, blue eyes. He seemed to have a glow about him, maybe it was just a trick of the light, but at that moment a thought flashed through my mind and gave me such a jolt…'This man looks just like Jesus!'

I brought him home with me and after eating and showering he slept on my couch. I left one of my shirts, a pair of jeans with twenty dollars in a pocket, a jacket, socks and a pair of old sneakers on the floor beside the couch and went to bed. I woke the next morning and found that the stranger was gone. On the coffee table lay a large manila envelope. He had written part of a short poem using a pencil, in a childlike scrawl on the back of the envelope. At the bottom he wrote, "Thank you for your kindness. I wrote this for us and I'm leaving it for you to finish. Until we meet again," Gabriel Molloy.

Mars Bars and Scars

Dreaming of the planet Mars,

Wistfully thinking upon fallen stars.

We found ourselves behind prison bars,

Me and Jesus, showing our scars and

remembering the magical nights

in those wild Irish bars.

Searching for paradise, our souls on ice,

choosing virtue over vice.

We remake the divine sacrifice

by being all too human,

me and Molloy.

Traveling through time and space

seeking the original universe,

and finding a sacred place

to sing of the blessings

and to nurse the curse.

See how to be.

Let the light set you free.

Eternal now,

shining into the black and blue void

on this good, godly night.

Live and let live is all there is,

the road less traveled *he* chose,

having no choice.

To become the ultimate sacrifice

For me and Molloy.

For Gabriel

Mars

In My Blood

Must I bleed all over the page
and purge my soul for all to see?
Rend open wide the deep dark rage,
will I then regain my sanity?
The mind in a whirl and racing
like a heartbeat bursting free.
Expel the thoughts, pain embracing
when once a story comes to be.
Can these words fulfill my need,
uncoil the depths of disparity?
Or bind me fast on endless seas
with roiling thoughts and fantasy.
Blood must spill across the page
or else coagulation rules.
If not expressed, this hidden rage
will blind and smite us all as fools.
Once heart's blood has poured clear through
relief will come and pain abate.
Released from fear if what I do,
is tell the tale with honest faith.

The Blank Page

We writers are a funny breed,
in search of thought and fertile seed.
To tell it all; a driving need,
and get it down at lightning speed.
It's good, it's bad, we can't agree,
must leave it for posterity.
A pencil, pen maybe a reed,
to conjure up the words we need.
Hair pulled out thrown on the floor,
scream and stomp, run out the door.
For inspiration rant and roar,
my head hurts now and I am sore.
The page is blank five whole weeks now
and sweat has risen upon my brow.
I want to write but don't know how
givin' up, goin' back to the plow.
But wait! What's that yonder callin' me?
A thought has come to set me free.
A glimpse of perfect poetry,
a writer now I'll surely be.

Those of us who have the gift of words should always use them to inspire and encourage others. While we must impart the truth, we should never be tempted to use our words negatively. Truth, when added to or subtracted from is truth no more. Our words are meant to firstly, enlighten ourselves and secondly, to pass them on to others. Make no mistake, we who have the ability to take the chaotic thoughts, ideas and emotions and fashion them into meaningful and beautifully expressive works of art, can make the difference needed in the world at this time. This applies to both the written and spoken word and goes out to those misguided unfortunates who would take the lies, half-truths and innuendo, invent the rumor and then, from the safety of the shadows, instruct their minions, the rumor-mongers, to cause ill will and spread spite and falsehood in an already troubled world.

The Poisoned Pen

Watch out for the poisoned pen,
whose words will flash through time and space.
Catch you when sleep sets in
stare at you right in your face.

Perhaps a dream, could it be real,
did black magic assume the role?
With the devil was there made a deal,
now 'twixt and 'tween, a deep black hole?

Clever playmate in hidden space,
the motive will be ever unclear.
The hardened heart now out of place
with what was once thought so dear.

An ancient hurt has wounded deep,
with lies and infidelity.
So now can't ever let it sleep,
until the time it is set free.

Innocence is a lonely place,
young spirit should never adult be.
For Heart and mind must win the race,
to attain sublime eternity.

A tortured mind drives deep the nail
that crucifies both heart and soul.
Cry and moan, to the heavens wail,
for peace of mind and love for all.

So beware my friends, take my word,
of the poison pen's ink and might.
'Twill cut and slice just like the sword
and hurt you deep with its feral bite.

3

ON THE ANCIENTS

The 'Mayan Prophecy of the Fifth Sun' began on December 21st, 2012 at 11:11 am CST. On that day a significant galactic line up occurred. The Sun appeared to line up with the black hole (the dark rift) in the center of our Milky Way galaxy. This line up happens once every 26,500 years and could be observed from Juan Fernandez Island in the Pacific Ocean. It is seen as a warning for us that we must change our ways. The Mayans believed that this lineup means that we are no longer in the 'World of the Fourth Sun' but are not yet in the 'World of the Fifth Sun.' This is the time of 'in-between,' the time of transition, the time of Limbo, if you like. As we pass through this time of transition there will continue to be a colossal, global convergence of environmental destruction, social chaos, political upheaval, war, and ongoing major earth changes, i.e. earthquakes, volcanic eruptions, extremes of weather, ice storms, hurricanes etc. It will also appear as though those in charge have lost their rational minds.

Humanity will continue, but in a different way. Material structures will change. From this we will have the opportunity to be more human. We are living in the most important era of the Mayan calendars and prophecies. All the prophecies of the world, all the many varied traditions are converging now. There is no time for games. The spiritual ideal of this era is 'action.' Most of the other cultures, including the Egyptians, the Minoans and even the Hopi Indians were given all of this information down through the ages, but it appears that the Mayans had the deeper knowledge and ability to interpret it all most accurately.

Carlos Berrios, a Mayan tribal elder sums it up perfectly when he states, "Just now the dark side (the Powers That Be) is very strong, and very clear about what they want. They have their vision and their priorities clearly held, and also their hierarchy. They are working in many ways so that we will be unable to connect with the spiral Fifth World in 2012 onward. The dark power of the declining Fourth World (3114 B.C. - 2012 A.D.) cannot be destroyed or overpowered. It's too strong and clear for that, and that is the wrong strategy. The dark can only be transformed when confronted with honesty, directly and with open-heartedness. This is what will lead us to unity, and this is the key concept for the World of the Fifth Sun."

The Prediction

Ninety one steps on each side set,
and the number of sides is four.
Add the platform on the high crest,
then three sixty five is the score.

It has always been done in this very way,
the last count to keep evermore.
To separate night from the day,
the ancients who knew it for sure.

The ball court where life was mere play,
is silent and now used no more.
Where the ghost still holds its sway,
with bright, keen eyes, trained on the shore.

Their calendar holds bare truth sere,
in bactun, long count, and much more.
Of the future from this very year,
the way is now clear, they are sure.

The orbs in the heavens are near,
they now dance to the rhythm of time.
And so it becomes crystal clear,
when the Sun and the dark rift align.

If we don't find the path and reform,
the Ancients will not heed our plea.
We must learn to live as when born,
or on our heads a sad plight they'll decree.

The oceans will wash o'er the land,
and the heavens will darken and cry.
The earth it will shake to bare sands,
and the mountains will crumble and die.

Rae, Alistair. Chichen Itza. February 18, 2009. Web. 23 Sept. 2015.
<https://commons.wikimedia.org/wiki/File:Chichen_Itza_(3326547826.).jpg>.

Abanoub11, Photo of Monument in Egypt. 27 Sept 2015. Web. 16 Oct 2015.
https://commons.wikimedia.org/wiki/File:Abanoub11.jpg#filelinks

Valleys and Dust

I've been down in the old valley. *His* valley, the secret one.
The one where blown sand slices like slivers of obsidian.
Where silent passages wind and curl into an underworld of
immortals. Hidden, sealed forever in Canopic jars. Eternity
whispers aloud from hewn stones telling of our future and
their past. Mortals in bleached white shrouds of Linen,
wound, wrapped. Arms crossed, old bones strewn, forgotten,
again and again. Still, always the jackal, watching, seeing.
In his jaundiced eye, reflections of re-birth concealed,
then revealed like second skin. Dry and stiff, like parchment.

I've been down in her valley too. She with the piercing eyes
and the false beard, ruling in lieu, serene and wise with
immortal beauty. Carriage and mien royal, deified. The flail
across the crooked staff. And always Anubis, watching,
protecting forgotten spaces. I've been down in Sheba's vale,
now sundered and awash in a false sea. *He*, greatest son of Ra,
moved, taken, swamped with man's desire and vulgar greed.
The cavern silent, awaits and beckons the return.
Glyphs scored deep in pylon and obelisk rise up, up greeting
Ra, the holy one, the anointed. With feather and hearts'
ultimate test, Isis awaits in patient silence. Osiris ever present,
inviting to home, across the vast divide.

Canyons and Dust

I've been down in the sacred canyon. The one where the spirits keen aloudin the dark. Down where red dust swirls in the hot, dry wind with incessant erosion. Down where the parched wadis beseech the heavens for water, the pueblos, sad, scorched remnants. The one where, in ages past, the *Clovis* peoples wove their storage baskets.

Down where the hand hewn rock shelters bear witness to a dead existence, the enigmatic messages visible on the bare walls, a stark reminder. The pit houses gone, the kivas sundered, making way for the next brave tribes to dwell. Down where the stone blocks age and shimmer in the relentless heat, a silent testament to the once great Anasazi, *the ancient ones.*

Down where dry, brittled shards glint amid the junipers and lonesome canyon walls, baking in the scorched sand. Down where the coyote wails at night, longing, his forlorn cries echoing, lost in his mourning. Down where dense, shading forests once flourished, green and majestic. All gone now. Dust in the harsh, unforgiving wind.

Yet, if it is quiet and still and if the sun is still above the horizon, and if you are tuned to the other realm, you will absorb their presence as you walk among and marvel at what remains of their once, multi-level dwellings. All laid out in perfect symmetry and a mirror image of the Cosmos. A testament to their skillful hands and brilliant minds.

The stones, cut with exquisite detail and built with mathematical and astronomical precision, defy all understanding. You will be as one with the Great Spirit as the natural mystical energy, afloat on the air, tangible in its permeation, invades your senses, envelops you utterly and slowly draws you in, inviting you in to their world, a world long gone, across and beyond the vastness of space and time.

NASA, Chaco Canyon, New Mexico. Jan. 2007. Web. 6 May 2014.
https://commons.wikimedia.org/wiki/File:Chaco_Canyon_Pueblo_Bonito_digital_reconst
ruction.jpg

The Valley

I've been down in the swamp valley, the *place of reeds*, birthplace of the Gods. The one where the eagle grasped the serpent in its' taloned grip atop the flowering cactus. The one where the frightened refugees sought shelter, their old lands dead from violent, volcanic upheaval, forcing them to flee and be reborn in new hope of light.

Down where the *chinampas*, the raised beds, tamed the stagnant swamps and life began anew, blessed and fruitful. Where the water channels, dug deep, made travel by canoe possible. Down where the absence of fortification attested to the peaceful Utopia and selective cultural diffusion.
Down where *thin orange* pottery and exquisitely
crafted obsidian tools, honed by ancient hands, were sent out and utilized widely among all of the peoples.

Down where echoes of Totonac, Olmec, Toltec, Zapotec, Mixtec, Maya and Aztec blend and infuse with poignant permeation. Down where urbanism took hold defiantly, and proudly proclaimed its existence.

Down where the avenue stretches past *talud* styled pyramids of Sun and Moon and the temples reach to the heavens. Down where the feathered serpent rose skyward and soared in magnificent glory.

Hynes, Jack. View from Pyramide de la luna_Wikimedia Project. 29 May 2006.
Web. 23 Sept. 2015 https://commons.wikimedia.org/wiki/File:View from
Pyramide_de_la_luna.jpg.

The Charioteer

Rameses was so great and true, across the desert he did shine.

His love in finest cobalt blue, from Nubia, their fate entwined.

This maid will soon be shining bright, in the temple of the sun god

Ra. From Luxor in the sacred light, their love will spread afar.

Swept out in chariot fine and swift, his heart leapt strong with pride.

The Hittite from him now did drift, on the plain of Kadesh high.

And blood did seep upon the sand, crimson red the sad result.

The bold invader vanquished, a ghost in the swirling dust.

A fanfare blows and people swarm, when he returns to home.

His sloe eyed beauty on his arm, to ascend the royal throne.

The pylons and the city walls, bear witness to his great feat.

Hieroglyph and hypostyle hall, etched deep, they still entreat.

On obelisk and granite pure, his name is carved on high.

Along the Nile his spirit soars, Nefertari by his side.

From the delta far away up north, to the hills of old Sudan.

His memory is still of worth, and revered by everyman.

Lassinio, Carlo, Angellelli, Giuseppe, Cherubini, Salvador, Rosellini, Ippolito. Egyptian Chariot. 1832-1844. Web. 04 Apr. 2015.
https://commons.wikimedia.org/wiki/File:Egyptian_Chariot_(colour).jpg.

JOHN A. BRENNAN

Old Nubia

From high on top of Aswan dam,
with Nasser's lake wild and free.
My mind awhirl with their sad plan,
of old Nubia now, no more to be.

The riches gone, the people flee,
leave village and the land behind.
The water wide and deep, a sea,
to reinvent a new mankind.

Sheba's ghost it still flies high,
spirit walks 'thru the wide valley.
The temple on the high bank nigh,
becomes a relic and a memory.

Chagny, B.N. Sudan Meroe Pyramids 2001. Web. 12 Dec. 2014.
https://commons.wikimedia.org/wiki/File:Sudan_Meroe_Pyramids_2001.JPG.

4

ON LOVE AND LUST, LOST AND FOUND

The Swans

He glides across the smooth lakes' surface, but she is nowhere in sight. Stately he moves on ever through the night. A moonbeam beckons to a hidden place where once they did dwell. *Faster* now, maybe she lays there, and love again might they share. But no earthly sign now, only pain. Mute, and no sound escapes. The reeds and rushes lay empty. The archer with arrows more plenty, has struck in her hearts' place. He follows the fading silver beam upward, up toward the eternal light.

The lake is quiet now, now that the swans have gone. Once they sailed its wide surface, silent and free. A ghostly presence is all that lingers on, to remind us of what there used to be. He searched for her, but alas, no trace, no sight. Meshed together now, mid the moons' clear light. His last song silent sung, from deep within. Then, merging slowly with the mist, he fades from without.

She

Among the saviors she resides
in quiet assurance of her place.
Lithe and languid, with regal mien,
she glides 'thru air bearing gift of life.
The mantle, flowing through the ages,
envelops her in verity profound.
Gently musing all the while,
in soft tones of measure, knowing.
The voice, breath soft in sublime
caress, whispers, *it's all good* and
good as so ever sought, sighs.
Her fair abstraction, niched in
careful frame, illuminates the
recess where the wayward
seeker dwells.
The essence of comfort, awaits its
release from restraint of time, space
and ethereal sublimity.

For Jennifer.

A French Girl's Kiss.

It started off in reminisce, a sultry look, a French girl's kiss.

The story born in London town, as Brian Jones went heaven bound.

Posted soon on a new web site, a review and then, she saw the light.

Her heart and soul would now ignite, juices flow, then she shines bright.

So long in dark and soulless place, buried deep, and the world not face.

The burning bush is now with grace, she longs for his complete embrace.

Of love and lust they speak aloud, desire to couple loud and proud.

Time and space block and cloud, they must wait for time allowed.

When these two meet and savor air, pure love will truly save this pair.

Old souls unite: it's come to pass, the magic blend will bind them fast.

Coupled with their hearts and trust, mix and join their love with lust.

A union forged on the astral plane, will now soar high and never wane.

Whispers

Whispering deep desires in the dark of night.

Enticing with smooth, sultry coaxing

and throaty promises.

Detailed and explicit, forcefully wanton.

Overwhelming.

Unfettered with lust and carnal desires.

Floods of passion course through the air

from far off place space and time.

Full of orgasmic excitement and need.

In glorious colored likeness,

open, inviting, so plain to see.

Wet with swollen invitation and want.

Gorged with blood, set on fire,

hot eyes pleading for the great release.

Then, lets it go…

The Lovesick Fool.

Love will come at the speed of light,

or creep up like the thief in night.

Catch you with most dreadful fright

make you think, 'am I alright?'

You sweat you quake, you sit and stand

you run you walk, was this planned?

I will, I won't, Shit! I don't know,

a drink might help, just let it flow.

A racing heart we all agree,

will set it off, one two three.

We babble wild and crazily,

the doctor we must surely see.

No pill for this, must let it be,

I think I've lost my sanity.

That siren call won't set me free,

'til I beg her please to pity me.

Is it real or a waking dream

I look the same but I just can't seem

to cure myself so I must come clean

And ask her if she'll be my Queen.

The Lovers

I sat alone to contemplate,
a voice that calls me to my fate.
Comes soft in dusk, at twilight's gate,
its mournful call will not abate.

Of war and peace and love and hate,
and heart and lust, the wild floodgate.
Mind and soul will meet, then mate
if not, then we must instigate.

The heavens part, expose their might,
of star-crossed lovers and their plight.
Cry and mourn in depth of night,
on bended knee, to seek insight.

Love will not come 'till we fulfill,
each other's needs, yet even still,
the banshee's cry, the night does fill,
with fractured hearts, and love for nil.

For what is love, that will not rhyme?
Fey juice aglow, her gardens shine.
Ripe seeds must flow into her prime
locked in embrace and then she's mine.

A tortured haunt with lust's cruel will,
twists me, turns me, just until,
she will relent, let love fulfill,
only then does fortune's plan instill.

JOHN A. BRENNAN

The Maid from the Glade

Aware he became of a girl in mist,
a whisper in time and a fey maid fair.
Far off in salty clime and mountain's kiss
calls out to him 'oer the soft clear air.

Soon he forgets all that went before now
only she can slow his lust and greed for her.
Show him how to meld with love sublime
and make his rest of time last forever.

Her breast is firm and young and will be sweet
of this he knows, but wants to cup them now.
Stave off the painful, it's not yet complete
'till she favors him and only then will endow.

To possess her, his drive is rampant high,
desires to enter her soul in the glen, hear her sigh.

The Game

They chanced across time and space,

stumbled playing the game within the game.

Fun and tease, of love they were bare,

testing their power over others,

to assure that it was still alive.

Kindred were the thoughts of what could be, a

dream with possibility and aching desire.

Confusion holding them back from the edge

scared to step off and free fall out,

out into the dark, fearsome void.

The hermit now returns to the forest

to be lone and heal the mind,

He waits in his death sublime and still.

Surrenders his soul to her free will.

Jealousy

Their love was gifted from on high.
Their pulsing hearts could kiss the sky.
Never more to part, and each to try,
deep and strong, and together fly.
Soar high and wide and ever be,
in trance and deep tranquility.
Pledge souls unite for eternity,
nothing now 'tween she and me.
From away out there in the blue
a monster with a vile green hue,
reared its head and then they knew,
jealousy was the winner true.

Betrayal

She felt betrayed by foolish me,

and hurt inside, was mad and sore.

I did not mean for this to be,

now she has shut and barred her door.

Once open wide and free it shone,

with love light and sweet harmony.

But now there's nothing at all warm,

only faded distant memory.

He wonders if she'll speak to him,

forgive him his idiocity.

And tell him that her love he'll win,

then give to him her hearts door key.

Pan

Fear, lust and greed enslave the soul.

The roman goat of illusion and extremes

will dance with you but leave you cold.

Greek god Pan is the playmate it seems.

Temptation rears and blinds the mind

with depth of pain as a cruel friend.

Hold fast to heart and Temperance find,

then slavery fades and love you mend.

Guilt dread cold with painful moan

is grasping at your earth mother's core.

A Fool of innocence once all alone,

is now renewed with a soul that soars.

The Saxon girl

With silken skin and warm to the touch

she came to me in the old Dutch barn.

A love of natural and the spoken word

were the threads to bind and sustain.

Hair as silver as the glowing moon

a smile on her so young and fair.

A gentle soul in the cool of the evening

walked with me through the shimmering air.

With piercing mind and aware of self

my hand she took as if we were lovers.

All fell away as we heeded the call

of Fate and the fortune that covers.

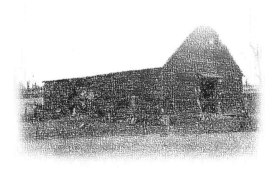

The Astral Plane
A cautionary tale regarding romance via the ether.

I once knew a girl from BC,
through the ether, she flew onto me.
She looked quite divine, a reviewer sublime,
and her stars she showered, with glee.

A lusty young maid, said she lived in a glade,
and me she was dying to see.
I was taken aback, with Canadian *craic*
and wondered if she was free

"Oh! Free as a bird," she said with a purr,
"I can't wait to sit on your knee.
I've fallen for you, my virile young sir
I'm panting profusely, you see.

I want to melt in your arms, let you sample my charms
I have many, as you'll come to see.
But first we must meet, each other to greet,
only then is it ever to be."

"But how can that be? You're in BC,"
I asked her one morning at three.
Astral plane, her reply, with a glint in her eye,
then I knew it never would be.

I like my mares at hand, and closer to me,
so I can tend to them every day.
It's easy to play, when they're not far away.
then most happy will I ever be.

Up there in the clouds, I just cannot see,
a mare being charming to me.
I'd rather her down, here on the ground,
easier to saddle, you see.

The Archer and the Scorpion.

The archer let her arrow fly,
and the scorpion she did sting.
From far off land of sea and sky,
has now made the heavens ring.
He was not sure if it could be,
but her aim was tried and true.
The fateful day when he did see,
the bolt from out of the blue.
He's different now and oft does swell,
with pure love for the maiden fey.
And he hopes that soon time will tell,
their love is no longer mere play.
Spans air and space in dream sublime,
their lust must be hard held at bay.
Till the angels set forth the time,
then archer and scorpion can play.
They dared to hope, the dream alight,
as in past times 'twas not true.
But the archer with her keen insight,
met the scorpion, and then she knew.
In Central park there is a glen,
where both of them will meet.
Not far is it from Shakespeare's pen,
'neath Cleopatra's high seat.

Blue Moon

All gone, without a trace to show,

  as if it never had been there.

At first the heart was all aglow,

but left too soon, with not a care.

Blue moon binds tight within its grasp,

pulls and tugs at deep inner core.

A roiling swirl and fear its clasp,

  break free or else the heart is sore.

The outer form is clear to see,

inner self hidden from view.

River deep and dark as the sea,

will wash away and at once renew.

Damaged souls are never free,

until they seek and find the source.

Be rid of anger and hostility,

eclipse of reason and its course.

So close and yet so far unfair,

in solitude with troubled mind.

Are those thoughts beyond repair

alone, confused and almost blind?

To plunge the depths of what once was,

and regret what has now slipped by.

The simple plan out of the air

has faltered since and gone in time.

A glimpse he had, or so he thought,

in smoke filled room, with loud refrain.

Just a smile was all he sought,

to try and ease dull aching pain.

Searched high and low, all for naught,

a heart did break, yet once again.

'Till in a glen, from whence he sought,

and found his true love… no more rain.

Laurels and Eucalyptus

She could have come in through the bathroom window

It *was* open…but not her. Her proud carriage and her

dignified mien dictated otherwise.

She came straight in through the front door bearing her

laurel leaf of eucalyptus.

'For you,' she said 'because I love you.' A glowing aura

surrounded her face and her eyes shone with an intensity

usually reserved for poetry and writing, her passions.

'You can't always get what you want' she said.

I said 'I don't want much and if you try, sometimes

you get what you need.' She turned and offered me her coat.

Joe Cocker, with the tortured, haunted soul, sang 'It Feels like
forever.'

'That's our song' she said. And so it began…

From the start I told her to watch for the signs, to pay attention.

'I will,' she said as she traced her initials in the dust that lay on the

surface of the side table.

'This is a powerful time in our lives,' I said as we kissed.

And then I inhaled her breath.

'I've been looking for you all of my life' she said.

'Well, now you've found me' I whispered.

Plato was right, I thought.

Broken Wings

The broken wings always found me,
through ether and o'er vast sea.
Their hearts were sore and never would be,
unless true love could set them both free.

They cried with a pain felt so deep,
their spirits alone in cold sleep.
Their minds now forever to weep,
as the time began its wide sweep.

On wings of a colorful hue,
He calls from aloft, to be true.
And washes away in the blue,
their suffering souls, to renew.

Dore, Gustave, Illustration for John Milton's Paradise Lost. 1866. Web. 27 Feb. 20015.
https://commons.wikimedia.org/wiki/File:Pardise_Lost_1.jpg.

Empty Space

Her heart is sore and empty now with distant hurt and pain.

She wonders if it will abate and love she'll find again.

A tortured soul can never sleep, it will wander aimlessly.

A lovesick fool now holds the key only he can set her free.

The past must die and bleed complete, for hope to take its place,

then love must be invited in, to fill that empty space.

If not, then it will fester long and soul destroyed its fate.

The pain will be much stronger then, no key will open the gate.

The author and his mother. Circa 1969
Photo supplied by Author

Epilog

I discovered the Tarot many years ago and the first thing it taught me was that in essence, it represents a journey that we all must take. Starting with the innocent, naïve Fool and ending with the World.

Full Circle.

The Fool stepped off into void of night, free fall wind in his face.
His heart was light, new goal in sight, as he searched for his rightful place.
A Magician's wand had set him free, with lazy eight, threw wide the gate,
Then ushered him to go and see, the lady there enthroned in wait.
The Priestess smiled serene and wise, knowing all that there is yet to be,
She guides him with a wave of hand, his task, to seek the earth lady.
The Empress robed in golden shine, the mother of all infinity,
Told him about the father of time, her consort, and his guide to be.
Reason rules, emotion must wait, only then to find what he so seeks,
A teacher true he must ingrate, Priest and Fool must surely speak.
Inspiration will now become so true, divine from out of deep blue sky,
A choice he makes, and now a clue, just one heart be guided by.
A chariot ride will help him see, how next it is to come to pass,
Action now is a need, a plea, then Justice he will surely grasp.
Time alone in forest glade heals heart and mind with lantern bright,
Fortune, fate and destiny made, with thought and time and inner light.
The lions roar will soon be heard, and tension cloud his troubled mind,
But patience will subdue the sword, Sacrifice, the only thing to remind.
Death and rebirth save him now, the cycle is almost complete,
Temperance calms the aching brow, but the Devil he must gladly meet.
When that occurs a flash is due, the Tower falls and then it's clear,
A star shines bright with silvery hue, but Moons light comes with confusing fear. A golden Sun will warm him, plus, success is at his fingertips,
Embrace it well, and when he does, with Judgment he will come to grips.
The World awaits on his command, reward and peace will then set him free,
Now he must go and grasp the hand, through time and space, for eternity.

For Ellen, my Mother.

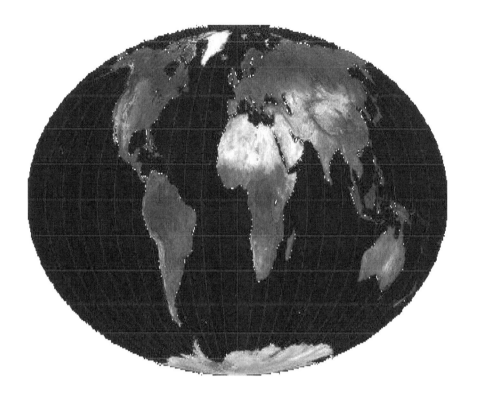

 ABOUT THE AUTHOR

Author John Anthony Brennan comes from Crossmaglen, a small, tough town in County Armagh, Ireland. A town like Ireland herself, which has endured and survived through the centuries, despite the influence of the invaders' harsh heel. He left his beloved, sacred green isle many years ago to explore the world, and has been island hopping ever since.

He has traveled extensively and visited many of the sacred sites. He incorporates his experiences in both his prose and poetry as he believes that a common thread connects us all. John is a member of the Long Island Writers Guild: The Amateur Writers of Long Island: The Performance Poets Association: Poets in Nassau, and the Bards Initiative. Much of his writing expresses the spiritual dimension and each piece hopefully contains a lesson coupled with historical facts.

His first book titled, **"Don't Die with Regrets,"** written to *hopefully* inspire others to **always** follow their dreams, has won the prestigious 2015 "Next Generation Indie Book" award in the Memoir category.

He is currently compiling a book of tribute poems dedicated to the musicians who, sadly, are no longer with us. Some of whom he met as a younger man living in London in the mid-sixties – mid-seventies.

My Journey

My Journey

My Journey

My Journey

My Journey

My Journey

My Journey

_____

_____

_____

_____

_____

_____

_____

_____

_____

_____

_____

_____

My Journey

_____

_____

_____

_____

_____

_____

_____

_____

_____

_____

_____

_____

_____

_____

My Journey

My Journey